PRAISE FOR *The*

T0268650

"For fifty years now, John Claypool has devoted himself to the care of souls. In this small but focused book, he offers the cumulative wisdom of those years to all whose hearts hunger for hope in a world that is running short on this ancient Christian virtue."
—Barbara Brown Taylor, author of *When God Is Silent*

"When you get a chance to hear John Claypool preach, you go. And when you get a chance to sit with him, you sit. Decades of pastoral and personal experience have combined to teach this renowned pastor a lot about what hope is and what it isn't, and have given him the wisdom to share it with us in simplicity and grace."
—Barbara Cawthorne Crafton, author of *The Sewing Room*

"*The Hopeful Heart* is a personal testimony, by one of the church's most inspirational storytellers, to his experiences with hope. It is an insightful meditative resource."
—John Westerhoff, author of *Will Our Children Have Faith?*

"*The Hopeful Heart* is a sensitive and important book. John Claypool, world-class preacher, steps out of the pulpit and leads us personally into the subterranean world of doubt and despair—where authentic hope is born. Whatever God may 'send' us, John helps us to recognize and receive the hope we long for."
—J. Keith Miller, author of *The Taste of New Wine* and *The Secret Life of the Soul*

OTHER BOOKS BY JOHN CLAYPOOL

THE
HOPEFUL
HEART

THE
HOPEFUL
HEART

John R. Claypool

Church Publishing
NEW YORK

Church Publishing
19 East 34th Street
New York, NY 10016
www.churchpublishing.org

Cover design: Corey Kent

Library of Congress Cataloging-in-Publication Data

Claypool, John.
  The hopeful heart / John Claypool.—1st ed.
      p. cm.
    ISBN: 978-0-89869-219-8 (pbk.)
    1. Hope—Religious aspects—Christianity. I. Title.
  BV4638 .C54 2003
  234'.25—dc21   2002153478

To my beloved wife, Ann, who fills my heart with hope,

and our cherished children and grandchildren,

Rowan, C.T., Laura, Marty, John, and Ashley

Contents

Acknowledgements

One of my favorite mentors was fond of saying that only God is into originality—the rest of us are merely passing on to others what was graciously given to us first. Saint Paul was very insightful in asking, "What do you have that you did not receive?" The answer, of course, is absolutely nothing at all.

Many are the givers by whom I have been graced in the writing of this book. In all honesty, however, one person above all others must be singled out for special acknowledgement and that is my soul mate, dearest friend, and loving wife, Ann. After my retirement from Saint Luke's Episcopal Church in Birmingham, Alabama, in 2001, the handling of most of the details of my life and work has fallen on her and I can never adequately acknowledge all she has done with me and for me. After my valued secretary at Saint Luke's, Marjorie Swanson, faithfully typed the oral transcripts of many of the presentations on the subject of hope that I had made across the years, Ann helped me in the direct shaping of this manuscript. It would not be an exaggeration to identify her as the co-author of this work, for her exquisite taste and feel for words have greatly enriched the composition of these pages.

I am also indebted to a new friend and colleague, Debra Farrington. Our lives crossed providentially this last summer at Kanuga Episcopal Retreat Center in North Carolina, and it was her encouragement and editorial assistance that brought this little volume to fruition. It is consistent with the theme of this book to hope that some of these words through the mystery of the printed page will be life-giving and authentically empowering to those who pay me the compliment of reading them.

John R. Claypool
October, 2002

THE
HOPEFUL
HEART

CHAPTER ONE

An Introduction

For a long time now, I have been drawn by a desire to explore more extensively the reality of hope. Bishop William Frey has described hope as "the Cinderella sister" of Saint Paul's famous trilogy of virtues in 1 Corinthians 13, because while voluminous attention has been focused on the subject of faith and love across the centuries, the subjects of hope has not been treated with equal seriousness. All you have to do to confirm this observation is to visit any large theological library and see the disproportion in the number of volumes on these three vital subjects. I am at a loss to account for this disparity of interest, for in my experience hopefulness is clearly as crucial for the living of life as either faith or love. I view hope as the very fuel that animates our human species and, as I will be contending throughout this volume, what breath is to the physical body, hope is to the human spirit.

I once heard wise people described as those who know what time it is in their own lives and in the life of the culture in which they are embedded. There is a tremendous potency in good timing, in sensing what is most appropriate to say and to do at a given moment and, while I would shy away from using the adjective "wise" to describe myself, I do have a profound sense that now is the time to share my thoughts on hopefulness that make up the following manuscript.

Like you, my life experiences have cast me in a wide variety of roles—those of son, husband, father, pastor, teacher, and just plain struggling human being. From every one of these angles, I have sensed not only the crucial importance of hope, but also how differently it is perceived and appropriated as the contexts of our lives change. In an effort both to experience and to share this life-giving reality, much of the material in the following chapters has been shaped and reshaped as I have submitted my notions for correction to countless others and encountered new insights that called on me to relinquish the old and embrace the new.

Those who have participated in the churches I have served since 1953, or who have been a part of innumerable teaching missions of mine across the years, will recognize many familiar themes and stories that I have never tired of sharing. While this volume represents the best that I know at this moment, the material has evolved through many forms and represents a long process of give and take and unnumbered revisions. I am under no illusion that what I have written is the last word on the mystery of hopefulness. There is always much yet to be learned. However, I would be pleased if what follows becomes the beginning of a new phase of your own thinking on hope.

My other reason for writing these words now has to do with the condition of our American culture. We are still reeling from the impact of the destruction of the World Trade Center and the attack on the Pentagon. We have been jolted into the awareness that there are many folk in the world who would delight in wiping us off the face of the earth. If this realization were not enough to send terror to the depths of our psyches, an altogether different kind of threat has suddenly emerged from an internal source, namely, the discovery that so many of our time-honored institutions, such as the Roman Catholic Church and the corporations of America, are riddled with abuse and dishonesty. An astute observer of our culture said to me recently that what was coming to light about the corrupt condition of our national character may in the long run be more detrimental to our well-being than the terrorist threat from without. In such an atmosphere, the need for access to authentic forms of hopefulness seems more urgent than ever.

Two observations about hope lay a foundation for all that is to follow. The first of these is the conviction that hope is utterly essential for the well being of our particular species. What breath is to the physical body, hope is to the human spirit. Hope is what animates us. It is the fuel that energizes us, gets us up in the morning, and propels us through the day.

Years ago, I heard about an experiment conducted in the graduate department of psychology in a well-known university. The researchers wanted to identify those factors that make for dynamic coping. They filled two vats equally full of water, and placed a rat of comparable age and size in each one. Not surprisingly, the little creatures began to swim instinctively. The only difference between the two vats was that the top of one was sealed shut, while the other was left open. The rat in the sealed vat quickly sensed a diminishing supply of oxygen, saw no visible way of escape, gave up, stopped swimming, sank to the bottom, and drowned in less than four minutes. In contrast, the other rat, seeing the opening at the top and having unlimited amounts of oxygen available, swam for an incredible thirty-six straight hours until the experiment was stopped. The obvious conclusion is the inversion of the familiar aphorism, "As long as there's life, there's hope." The deeper truth is that "as long as there's hope, there's life." Hope is the reality that animates our particular species and the fuel on which our very life runs. Think about it: You would not have begun to read this book if you did not have some inkling that a positive prospect might be in the offing.

Another way of establishing the importance of hope is to think of those people you have known in the past who have somehow lost touch with hope and then consider the effect that this experience had on their lives. In his moving autobiographical book entitled *A Sacred Journey*, Frederick Buechner described the saga of his father's life. The elder Buechner was born into an affluent, achieving family in New York City. Three generations earlier, the elder Buechner family members had been radical free-thinkers who had come to America from Germany. While they were successful professionally and financially, they had disdain for the religious dimension of life. Frederick Buechner's father went to Princeton as an undergraduate, as had his father and grandfather. He did quite well and showed every promise of carrying forward the achieving family tradition when he was graduated in the mid-1920s. However, the Great Depression came along, and as a result he was never able to find and keep the kind of job that would have enabled him to provide well for his family. Unfortunately, he began to depend on alcohol as a way of coping with his feelings, which only exacerbated the problem. Then, early one Saturday morning in November of 1936, when young Frederick was only ten years old, his father got up before everyone else in the household, dressed and went down to the garage, carefully closed the door, turned on the ignition of his old Chevrolet car, sat down on the running board, and was asphyxiated before anyone in the family realized what was happening.

Years later, when people would ask Frederick Buechner how his father had died, he would always answer, "He died of heart trouble." He reflected that this was at least partially true for he had a heart and it was troubled, and at the bottom of that trouble was a deadly sense of hopelessness. I once heard the chaplain at a mental hospital say that the most common characteristic of the patients he served was this same malady of despair. Behind so many of the malfunctioning minds and spirits of these people was the feeling that there was no meaningful future to look forward to, no positive possibilities to draw them toward the Great Not Yet. Thus, my first observation is simply this: Hope is essential to us. What the breath is to our physical bodies, hope is to our human spirits.

My second observation is that, despite our crucial need for hope, there is nothing simple or magical about the act of hoping, for there is always the risk of disappointment. For example, the fact that I hunger for food does not, in and of itself, create nourishment, just as the fact that we very much need to hope does not automatically produce altars upon which we can safely rest our expectations. Think of the times that you have placed your hopes in a person, an institution, or a certain set of circumstances, only to see these hopes painfully dashed and crumble into dust. For there to be a hope that does not disappoint, it has to be reality-based. I like the definition of hope that Father William Inge gives in his book *Images of Hope:* "Hope sees that which is possible, but is not yet." In other words, hope senses the potential that exists in the realm of the real but has not yet been realized, and it moves toward the actualizing of these possibilities. There is a difference between the hopes that are connected with facets of reality and the kind of wild fantasies that have no roots whatsoever in actuality. Father Inge contended quite appropriately that hope is by no means absolute, for it has definite limits.

For example, it would be futile to hope that you could be born to different parents once you have already entered history or to hope that you will never die. To engage in such unrealistic expectations is to set yourself up for inevitable disappointment. This leads to the crucial question of where resources of hope can be found that can support our expectations. No inquiry could be of more urgent or primal importance, and the rest of this volume represents the best discoveries on this subject that I have made.

CHAPTER TWO

Avenues to Authentic Hope

The struggle we face now is how to have hope in a world that is littered with experiences of disappointment. As I have already noted, there is nothing simple or automatic about the act of hoping. The renowned poet T. S. Eliot once wrote:

I said to my soul, "Wait, but wait without hope,"
for to hope would be to hope for the wrong things.

Like most of us, Eliot probably had had experiences in which his positive expectations of some person or institution had been disappointed. One cynic has gone so far as to coin the aphorism, "Hope, as a rule, makes many a fool." How, then, do we set about discovering what we need so desperately in a context that is filled with so much risk and failure?

Verses from 1 Corinthians 13 suggest two potentially fruitful avenues to hopefulness that emerge from an understanding of our human nature. After his familiar description of love, Saint Paul goes on to say, "We humans know in part and we prophesy in part. . . . Now we see in a mirror, dimly" (1 Corinthians 13:8-13, KJV). These words break down into two very important affirmations, namely, that we do not know everything but, at the same time, we do know some things. I want to explore both of these aspects of our humanness. Taken together, I believe they can help us see the future as a friend, not a foe, and enable us to reach out expectantly to positive prospects yet to be experienced.

Acknowledging Mystery

The first step in understanding hope is to acknowledge the deep mystery that pervades all human existence, a mystery that should call forth in us a stance of genuine humility. Here we are, in a world that we did not create, surrounded by much that we neither understand nor comprehend. The Psalmist reminds us, "It is God who hath made us, and not we ourselves" (100:3), which is to say that we are radically contingent beings. After all, we did not will ourselves into this world, nor did we set in motion this incredible process of history in which we find ourselves. There is so much that makes up this existence of ours that we cannot explain, so much that we simply do not have the intellectual capacity to comprehend. Thus, the humility that is implied by saying, "We know in part and we see through a glass darkly," is actually an acceptance of the fact that mystery is the true context of our lives.

I remember vividly a glimpse into these two pathways to hopefulness given to me by a wonderful old Jewish rabbi, whom I had befriended in the turbulent 1960s. I need to confess that growing up in the southern way of life in Nashville during the 1930s and 1940s, I did not even realize that there was a racial problem in our culture. I embraced the way whites and blacks related to each other back then as an acceptable norm. However, in the fall of 1950, a man named Clarence Jordan came to the little college that I was attending, and in one week's time, he turned my perceptual world upside down and created for me what is often described as "the white man's burden." I realized that our segregated way of living was a contradiction, not only of our national ideals, but also of the heart of the gospel. From that time forward, I felt called to do what I could to achieve racial equality. All of my family's forebears were slave-owners, and this motivated me to try to be a part of the answer where I felt my kind had been part of the problem.

When I began to serve a church in Louisville, Kentucky, in 1960, I immediately aligned myself with groups that were working to heal our cultural sickness, and that is how I met this gracious old rabbi. We were an odd couple in many ways. He was in his seventies, and his family had been through the Holocaust in Eastern Europe. He knew much about the dark side of human existence while I, on the other hand, was very naïve and had not yet been initiated into the fraternity of the suffering. We were working together in the civil rights movement and, one afternoon, we participated in a very tense meeting with several African American ministers. They finally stormed out in a rage, accusing us whites of having no courage, and what began as a hopeful endeavor ended in total frustration. We happened to be meeting in this rabbi's synagogue, and as

I left, I said to him, "I think it is hopeless. This problem is so old, so deep, so many-faceted, there is simply is no way out of it." He responded by saying, "If you have a few minutes, I would like to talk to you about what you have just said." With that, he ushered me into his study and we both sat down.

I still remember how unhurriedly he lit his pipe and disappeared for a moment in a cloud of smoke. As the smoke began to dissipate, he said, "I need to tell you something, young man. To the Jew, there is only one unforgivable sin, and that is the sin of despair." He continued, "Humanly speaking, despair is presumptuous. It is saying something about the future that we have no right to say because we have not been there yet and do not know enough. Think of the times you have been surprised in the past as you looked at a certain situation and deemed it hopeless. Then, lo and behold, forces that you did not even realize existed broke in and changed everything. We do not know enough to embrace the absolutism of despair and, theologically speaking, despair is downright heretical. If God can create the things that are from the things that are not, and even make dead things come back to life, who are we to set limits on what that kind of potency may yet do?" That exchange occurred over forty years ago, yet here I am recounting these words once again because of the powerful impact they had on me. This is exactly what Saint Paul affirmed in his twofold depiction of our human situation, and that is how I came to believe that humility before what we do not know and acceptance of what we do know from Scripture can lead us into "the promised land" of hope.

One of my favorite writers, who knew both this humility and this acceptance as the pathway to hope, was the late Anthony De Mello, an insightful Jesuit priest from India. He spent his whole life gathering wonderful stories and modern parables from all the different traditions of the world. I am told that of the thousands of stories that he managed to gather, the one about an old Chinese farmer was his very favorite. It seems that this peasant owned a single horse on which he depended for almost everything. When it was time to plant in the spring, he would hitch the horse to a plow to break up the ground for the seeds. At the end of the growing season, he would hitch the same horse to a wagon in which he took the surplus to market. Whenever he was going to take a long trip, he saddled the animal, which then became his main vehicle for transportation.

There was hardly a day that went by when the horse did not figure significantly in the life of the old farmer.

One afternoon a bee stung the horse on its neck and, in panic, the animal ran away into the hills behind the farmer's house. The old man tried to head him off, but could not keep up, so as the sun went down that night, he had to go home and tell his wife that his beloved horse had run away. All of this took place in a tiny village in interior China where almost nothing exciting ever occurred. An event of this sort became a conversation piece for everyone. Wherever the old farmer went during the next week, his neighbors would shake their heads and say, "Sure sorry to hear about your bad luck, losing your horse," and the old man would shrug his shoulders and say, "Good luck, bad luck, who's to say?" A week later, to his absolute amazement, his beloved horse reappeared, accompanied by six wild horses he had met high up on the slopes, and the farmer was able to corral all of them, which was a great economic bonanza. Now, everywhere he went his neighbors would say, "Sure glad to hear about your good luck, getting all those horses," and he would shrug and reply, "Good luck, bad luck, who's to say?"

His son was anxious to make the most of this good fortune, so he began to try to break in these wild horses and to get them to the point of wearing bridles and saddles. However, he had never done this kind of work before, and because of his inexperience, he was thrown from one of the horses and broke his leg in three places. Word spread throughout the community, and everywhere the old farmer went for the next week, his neighbors would say, "Sure sorry to hear about your bad luck, your boy getting hurt," and characteristically, he would shrug and reply, "Bad luck, good luck, who's to say?"

Two weeks later, a war broke out between the city-states of interior China, and the army conscripted every able-bodied male under the age of fifty to go and fight. Of course, the farmer's son would have been in this category and would have had to go had it not been for his injury, and this proved to be fortuitous indeed, because every other villager who was conscripted wound up being killed in battle. As you have probably anticipated, when word spread of these events, his neighbors all said, "Sure glad to hear about your good luck, your boy being spared," and the old farmer shrugged once again replying, "Good luck, bad luck, who's to say?"

I believe that the reason De Mello loved this story so much is that it vividly reminds us that in any given moment we never know the full extent of what is happening about us. A depth of mystery pervades all of life and the only appropriate response is genuine humility and the willingness to admit, at least to oneself, "I may see what is happening before me, but my understanding of it is very partial indeed." The first avenue to hopefulness, then, is the admission that we do not know enough to embrace the absolutism of despair. The old rabbi was profoundly correct. Humanly speaking, despair is presumptuous.

Finding Hope in Scripture

We do not know everything, as Saint Paul tells us, but we do know some things and our Scriptures are an important source of what we can know. I believe we Christians are exceedingly graced by our exposure to the Great Story that courses through Holy Scripture. Frederick Buechner was correct in saying that we are no better than the Communists in China or the Buddhist peoples of the east, but we are simply luckier for having been exposed repeatedly to the scriptural accounts of the great love and mercy of the Divine.

What is the Great Story? You have probably heard it many times. It begins in that time before time when there was nothing except God, nothing except this Mystery that is life and has the power to give life. Sometime long ago, something utterly momentous must have happened in the heart of this Mystery we call God. The Mystery must have said, "This wonder of aliveness that I am is simply too good to keep to Myself. I want others to taste the ecstasy of being and having and doing. I want others to share in the utter joy of what I am and what I have." This constitutes the first movement in the Great Story of Holy Scripture, namely, the Holy One choosing to become the Generous One. You realize, do you not, that this is why all of us are here today. We did not call ourselves into being out of nothingness. As creatures, it is our nature to receive life, and if it were not for the generosity of the Holy One we would not exist, a word that means literally to "stand out of nothingness."

It is important to realize that God created, not to get something for God's self, but to give something of God's self. There was no emptiness in God that prompted this One to act out of self-regard, nor was there any outside force that coerced the Holy One to create. This momentous shift of the Holy One becoming the Generous One was purely intentional. God acted this way because it was God's deepest desire to share and to make the kind of joy that was essentially God's accessible to other creatures as well. This particular kind of joy was a very personal reality. It was a joy that grew out of freedom, the power to act, and the capacity to experience real delight from reflecting on what had been done. Neither a rock, nor a tree, nor any inanimate object can ever taste this sort of joy. This means that for humans to have the capacity for what God wanted us to experience, God had to give us the gifts of freedom and power.

However, giving us those gifts was a risk for God. If the recipients are authentically free, there is no anticipating how they are going to behave or use what they have been given. For reasons that are just as mysterious as the Holy One becoming the Generous One, the very creatures who had been called out of nothing proceeded to take this incredible gift and use it as if it were their own to do with exactly as they pleased. This meant that they arrogantly ignored the pattern of love that was the essence of God's kind of joy, and the result was a tragic unmaking of the kind of world that God called into being.

Scott Peck's young son said to him one day, "Have you ever noticed that the word 'evil' is the word 'live,' spelled backwards?" That statement also reflects a profound insight into what the Bible calls "the mystery of iniquity." There is no rational explanation of why creatures who were made for joy turn to senseless self-destruction, yet this is one of the primal characteristics of evil—it is a sheer absurdity, a form of action that makes no sense at all. God started with nothing and from chaos created form and beauty. Evil reverses that basic pattern by turning form and beauty back into chaos and, if it has its ultimate wish, back into the nothingness from whence it came. Here is the powerful "death-wish" that Sigmund Freud found buried in the depths of the human psyche. It represents the polar opposite of what the Generous One had intended from the very beginning.

The Bible is quite graphic in the way it depicts God's reaction to the human propensity for evil. The Generous One was clearly brokenhearted about the choices that his beloved creatures had made and, if you read the sixth chapter of Genesis carefully, God is depicted as expressing regret for having ever set out on this adventure of generosity. Like a jilted lover or betrayed parent, the Generous One descended into the abyss of grief and even entertained the thought of allowing the whole creation to dissolve back into the nothingness from which it had come. The drama of this particular moment is spelled out in suspenseful detail in Holy Scripture, as the Generous One came within a "hair's breadth" of abandoning this saga of history forever. However, at that juncture, something surprising and even miraculous occurred. The Creator saw a man, an individual named Noah, and somehow the original dream of God's joy becoming our joy was revived. In the face of these conflicting emotions, God decided on two courses of action. The first was to allow most of creation to have its way and return to nothingness. The flood represented a return of most of creation to the primordial watery chaos from which it had emerged. The other action was to gather together a fraction of creation and, in great compassion, to start all over again.

To fulfill that latter intention, God instructed Noah to build an ark and to preserve representatives of all that had been created. The "death-wish" was given free rein in a creation-wide destruction, but a remnant was saved through Noah and the blessed old ark. When the floodwaters subsided, another crucial movement in the Great Story proceeded to unfold. God seemingly passed a milestone by deciding to hang up "the bow of destruction" in the heavens, described in Genesis as "a rainbow," and God promised never again even to consider giving up on the original goal of sharing divine joy. Here the Generous One became the Merciful One and pledged to devote all future energies to the task of redeeming creation, rather than destroying it and abandoning the dream. This is a harrowing, breathtaking account of what happened within the heart of the Holy One, and this account lays the foundation for what has been called "the salvation history" of Israel.

God's next redemptive strategy was to show the world, through the legendary Father Abraham and his descendants, how wrong the serpent in the Garden of Eden had been in accusing the Holy One of being untrustworthy. When the Holy One said to Abraham, "I want to bless you," God was simply restating why he had ever chosen to create at all. Remember, the desire to share God's kind of joy was what prompted the adventure of history in the first place. In the story of Abraham, that intention reasserts itself even more powerfully than before. It was one thing to act in a spirit of pure generosity toward humankind. It was an even more awesome phenomenon to continue such an endeavor in the face of humanity's blatant ungratefulness and destructiveness.

Across many centuries, the Merciful One struggled to help people realize that "God is light, and in him is no darkness at all." In the fullness of time, God decided on yet another redemptive strategy, which was to send the very heart of God's nature into history in the form of a single human being, Jesus of Nazareth. This One was the beloved Son of God, sent into the world to reveal God's essence in a flesh and blood embodiment, a task he performed flawlessly. As Saint Augustine once observed, "Jesus loved each one as if there were none other in the world to love, and he loved all as he loved each." It is hard to decide which aspect of such affection is more amazing, its individualized intimacy or its all-inclusive scope; but these qualities were both apparent in the personhood of the Nazarene who "became flesh and dwelt among us."

Regrettably, however, that same old bentness of spirit and arrogant rejection of the role of creatureliness surfaced again, and the mystery of iniquity, in all its awesome destructiveness, attacked Jesus in full force. We responded to the best thing God had ever done for us by doing the worst thing possible. We took this expression of God's love and treated him in ways that we would not treat a mad dog. We abused the most loving human who had ever lived among us in the most unloving fashion. We scoffed at him, made fun of him, taunted, tortured, and finally crucified him so that he died in the most shameful and humiliating of ways. I have to believe that, on the night of that first Good Friday, when Jesus was reduced to a bloody corpse in a borrowed grave, God's "rainbow resolve" never to give up on us humans must have been tested as never before. What possible hope could there be for a species that was capable of this kind of blatant inhumanity?

I do not think the depth of this dilemma ever came clear to me until I became a father myself and experienced what one feels for "bone of one's bone and flesh of one's flesh." I am graced with having a son, who is both my namesake and the object of my deepest affection. If any group of human beings ever did to my own child what the world did to Jesus, treating him as inhumanely as Jesus was treated in his last days—even if I possessed the power to raise my boy back from the dead, I would never consider sending him back to those who had treated him so horribly. I would be so filled with rage at the hideousness of this crime that I would want to blast them back into nothingness for eternity.

However, as I live into these feelings of such anger, the true miracle of Easter breaks over me with startling power. The wonder of that particular event was not just that God *could* bring back to life what had been so brutally killed, although that in itself is an astonishing potency. No, the greater miracle is that God *would want* to do so at all, or would have any hope or affection left for a species that had shown itself to be capable of such mindless destruction and brutality. However, God's response on Easter was the climax of the Great Story that courses its way throughout all of Holy Scripture. Not even the killing of God's Son could kill the desire of God to share divine joy with the entire human race. The Mystery who stands behind all of reality is an Easter Being, which is why my friend the rabbi was even more insightful than he realized when he said, "Theologically speaking, despair is downright heretical." If the crucifying of the heart of God's heart did not undo "the rainbow resolve," who are we to set limits on what the Merciful One might yet do with all we have done to God's beloved creation?

My contention, then, is quite simple: a hope that will not disappoint is possible if you choose to join all that you do not know about reality with all that you do know from the implications of the Great Story of Holy Scripture. Humility and revelation together form avenues to authentic hopefulness. I invite you to embrace them both.

31

CHAPTER THREE

What Can We Expect of God?

I ended the last chapter with the suggestion that a certain understanding of the nature of the Holy One is at least one of the avenues by which we can gain access to the kind of hope that will not disappoint us. In this chapter, I would like to elaborate on the idea that opening ourselves confidently to the workings of the God of Holy Scripture is a way to experience that which has the power to energize our lives. Father William Inge contends that hope is profoundly relational, not simply an internal activity of the mind. For hopefulness to become a reality, there must be something beyond ourselves with which we can collaborate and on which we can depend. It is interesting to note that our English words "hope" and "help" are derived from the same basic root. There are still pockets of culture, such as in the Appalachian mountains of Kentucky, where the words are used interchangeably. For example, when people from this area ask, "Can you hope me out?" they are really reaching out for help. We need to reach out to God in the same way.

Holy Scripture abounds in positive promises about the reality of such helpfulness. The Psalmist describes God as "our refuge and our strength, a very present help in time of trouble" (Psalm 46:1). Saint Paul goes so far as to claim that "God will supply all of our needs according to his riches in glory" (Philippians 4:19). The prophet Isaiah wrote, "They who wait upon the LORD shall renew their strength. They shall mount up with wings as eagles. They shall run and not be weary. They shall walk and not faint" (Isaiah 40:31). If these words mean anything at all, the implication is that the Mystery we call God can be counted upon to meet us in the details of everyday life and to do tangible things on our behalf. The writer of the book of Hebrews describes this phenomenon as "the grace to help us in our times of trouble" (Hebrews 4:16). The question becomes: What form does this saving help assume amid the concrete circumstances of our lives?

Our expectations play an important role in how we perceive reality. This fact was brought home to me quite dramatically years ago when I first read C. S. Lewis's little book entitled *A Grief Observed*. Lewis had been a bachelor until, at fifty-six years old, he married an American Jewish woman named Joy Davidman, whom he came to love quite profoundly. What he had not been given in his twenties and thirties, he wrote, was graciously bequeathed to him in his fifties, and he came to delight in this gift of marriage. Lewis's bride had miraculously recovered from cancer just after they were married, but following three years of delightfully satisfying bliss, the cancer returned and she died in a matter of weeks. Lewis was devastated by this sudden turn of events, and was cast into the valley of the shadow of grief.

Lewis kept a personal journal throughout his lifetime, and in the weeks following his wife's death, he recorded his feelings and fears during that period of overwhelming loss. Not long before his own death, he was persuaded to publish this portion of his journal as *A Grief Observed*. The book begins on about as shrill a note of religious disappointment as I have ever encountered. Lewis made no effort to hide how utterly betrayed he felt by the God he had come to know and trust. He had expected certain consolations to emerge from his faith but, to his great dismay, they had not materialized when he first found himself in the depths of sadness. He exploded in a volley of verbal invectives, accusing the Holy One of being cruel, or even worse, a totally sadistic torturer. Lewis sounded like a person who had been betrayed by false promises or shamelessly "sold a bill of goods." He unpacked his frustrated heart as only a master wordsmith can do.

However, as Lewis continued to wrestle with God, a new possibility emerged. He began to realize that his sense of betrayal might have been caused more by his expectations than by what had actually occurred. He had mentally constructed the forms of consolation he expected from God ahead of time and when these did not unfold as he had anticipated, he responded in fiery indignation. He proceeded to do what the well-known mystics have always advocated, which was to cleanse the lenses of his expectations before coming to any conclusion. When he did this, what he discovered was that God had been present all along and had in fact provided consolations, but because they were different from the ones Lewis expected, he had failed to perceive them initially. When he looked back on the weeks that followed his wife's death and focused on what had actually happened, he saw more clearly the presence of the Divine. As a result, *A Grief Observed* ended on a far more hopeful note than it began.

I first read this book in the late 1960s and, when I put it down, a holy hush came over my whole being. At the time, I was an active pastor, and what came to me was the awesome challenge of handling responsibly the promises of God. I have already mentioned the numerous positive expressions of hope that fill the pages of Holy Scripture, and I found myself asking, "How can I articulate these realities to people without setting them up for the forms of disappointments that can so easily develop?" I have been pondering this question for over thirty years now, and I have come to the conclusion that the secret lies in realizing that God's "grace to help us in our times of trouble" comes not in exclusively one form but actually in three distinct manifestations. The way to avoid the pitfalls of disappointment is to include all three of these forms in constructing our spectrum of expectation. What, then, are these three components of a hopeful perspective?

God and Miracles

The first category consists of what I would call events of intervention, rescue, and miracle. There are times when, for God's own inscrutable purposes, God chooses to break in from a transcendent dimension and alter the circumstances in which we find ourselves. An illustration of this is found in Mark's Gospel when a pathetic leper approached Jesus and said, "If you will, you can make me clean" (Mark 1:40). The text says that Jesus was "moved with pity" at the sight of this one and proceeded to respond in two ways. First, he did the unthinkable in that culture by reaching out and touching the diseased man. Then he said simply: "I will; be clean" (Mark 1:41). In the twinkling of an eye, energies from another dimension of reality broke into that situation and, in astonishment, the leper saw his body restored to wholeness. The One who had created the world out of nothing chose to recreate a broken portion of it in a matter of seconds.

What we are encountering here is that mysterious realm of the miraculous. I do not know how you feel about such phenomena, because over the last four hundred years our western world has grown more and more skeptical of such possibilities and you may have also. The scientific approach to understanding reality tends to crowd out any serious regard for the category of the miraculous. However, I have been greatly enlightened by something that Saint Augustine wrote many centuries ago. He claimed that what the Bible calls miraculous has more to do with timing than with anything else. According to Augustine, miracles are those moments when, for reasons of God's own, the Holy One chooses to do quickly what that One usually does at a more deliberate pace. As an example, Augustine pointed out that water is always being turned into wine in the slow unfolding of the agricultural seasons. A grape seed is planted in the ground; rain falls and swells that seed, which then sends up a shoot. That shoot eventually develops leaves and fruit and, in due time, that fruit swells with water and ripens. The grape is then harvested and put into a vat and pressed. Over a period of months or years, water turns into wine. However, at the wedding feast in Cana of

Galilee (John 2:1-11), when Jesus turned vats of water into wine, the Holy One chose to do quickly what usually happens at a more deliberate pace.

Augustine saw the same pattern at work in the story of Jesus multiplying the loaves and fishes in the wilderness (Matthew 14:13-21). Each spring, when a farmer plants seeds and carefully nurtures the wheat crop until the harvest, and every time fish swim back upstream to spawn, loaves and fishes are multiplied. However, the day Jesus faced five thousand hungry humans, God chose to do instantly what usually takes place more slowly. What I like about this interpretation of miracles is that it reminds us of the mysterious character of all experience. That anything develops out of nothingness (which is what our English word "exist" actually means) is a towering miracle. The fact that things *are* is a greater mystery than how slowly or quickly they came to be.

The twentieth-century theologian Paul Tillich claimed he was awakened to his philosophic quest by the most ultimate of all questions: "Why something and not nothing?" If you look at that mystery long enough, you may come to the conclusion that, between the conditions of non-being and being, there is one connecting link that many of us dare to call "God." In this view of reality, everything literally hangs like a chandelier on the single fact that God wanted it to be and had the power to create it out of nothing. Thus, I do believe in the possibility of miracles, those times when things happen for which there is no human or physical explanation. These are the kind of events that leave us with what an old friend of mine used to call "slack-jawed amazement."

Having affirmed my belief in the possibility of miracles, however, there are two other considerations to be addressed. The first is that what we all hope for initially when we find ourselves up against difficult circumstances is some form of the miraculous, and there is a good reason for that being our first instinctive desire. Our first experience of help assumed the form of intervention and rescue. At birth, when we are virtually helpless in every way, crying was the only means we had to make our neediness known, and if the big people around us had not responded in some form of practical caring, then we would not have survived. You and I are monuments to the reality of intervention and rescue. Someone picked us up, washed us off, fed and nurtured us in ways that we could not do for ourselves, and these experiences made a primal impression on our psyches. Therefore, it is not surprising that when we encounter such helplessness once again, the old memory revives and we long for God to do what the big people did for us in our infancy.

This means that, regardless of our age, we should not be surprised or ashamed to find ourselves praying for a miraculous rescue from some problem situation. It is significant to me to note that when Jesus was at the height of his maturity and within hours of his own death, he said the same thing to his Father in heaven that the leper had said to him years before. There, in the Garden of Gethsemane, as he faced the horrific prospect of being tortured and killed, Jesus prayed, "Father, all things are possible to you. Please take this cup from me." It is perfectly understandable to cry out for miracles when we are really up against it.

The other consideration is that, while I do believe in the miraculous, miracle is not the only form of action that is worthy of the adjective "divine." I fear that today's television evangelists have talked so much about expecting miracles that they have given the impression that spectacular healings are the only way God works in our world. This perspective sets the stage for real disappointment. As firmly as I believe that God does choose to intervene miraculously on occasion, I am equally convinced that this does not exhaust God's repertoire of redemptive strategies. As I survey Holy Scripture and the long centuries of church history, I sense two other ways that God proves to be "our refuge and strength," and these two must be added to the possibility of miracle as valid keys on the keyboard of God's caring responses.

God and Collaboration

The second form of God's "grace to help" is collaboration or partnership. Occasionally, God chooses to break in and solve our problems for us, but at other times God moves alongside us and invites us to join forces with him in bringing about a solution to our difficulties. Our identity as co-creators becomes a reality when this happens. We are offered the opportunity of combining our skills, insights, and energies with those of God to resolve our problems.

A good example of this is found in Exodus, the second book of the Old Testament. Exodus provides a wonderful account of how the Hebrews were delivered from their bondage in Egypt. During Joseph's rise to power centuries before, they had migrated to Egypt from Palestine, but political conditions have a way of shifting and the Egyptians had become very uneasy with the presence of the Hebrews among them. The Egyptians were intent upon keeping the number of Hebrews from growing, and to that end they issued an edict that every male Hebrew baby should be killed at birth. Moses, the chief figure in the Exodus saga, was born during this anguished and torturous time. Somehow, his mother managed to evade the authorities and keep the tiny infant alive. Since she was a slave who had to go to work everyday, she devised an ingenious plan. She lived near the Nile River and made a little bamboo float into which she placed the infant Moses. She nestled this float among the bulrushes so it would not be seen and assigned her oldest daughter to keep a watchful eye on it while she was away each day. One morning, by what I call providence rather than coincidence, Pharaoh's daughter came to the river to bathe. Just at that moment, the infant cried and the royal princess discovered him. In a moment of impulsive affection, Pharaoh's daughter resolved to adopt this tiny infant in defiance of her father's dictum. At that juncture, Moses' resourceful sister entered the scene and said, "I know a wonderful woman who would be glad to help you take care of this baby"—referring, of course, to

Moses' birth mother. The proposition appealed to the royal princess, and with his own mother as his caretaker, Moses was exposed to his Hebrew heritage and learned what it meant to be a part of the chosen people who were descended from Abraham.

As Moses grew older, he was educated as a prince of Egypt and was given incredible opportunities and privileges. However, the dilemmas of his dual background began to emerge as he became an adult. I once heard that there are only two kinds of people in this world—those who want to make the world a better place for everyone and those who are content to make a better place for themselves in the world as it is. If Moses had been of that latter persuasion, he would have forgotten all about the slaves who were his natural forebears and taken his good fortune for granted. However, he turned out to be of that rare and noble breed that genuinely cares about everyone and so he could not bear to see people being oppressed. He resolved to do something about this situation but, like so many naïve adolescents, he tried to "cut the Gordian knot" of social injustice by a single act of violence. Witnessing an Egyptian overlord mistreating a Hebrew, in a fit of righteous indignation Moses killed the abuser with his own hands. I suppose that Moses thought this action would spark a revolution and that the Hebrews would rise up as one against the Egyptians, but these downtrodden slaves did not even know who Moses was since he had lived most of his life in the palace. The Egyptians were enraged when this outsider who had been given so many royal advantages suddenly turned into a revolutionary and became an enemy of the state. The word went out that this ingrate must be put away and, in order to save his life, Moses fled into the desert.

Suddenly, the bottom dropped out of Moses' life and, for all his royal education, he was reduced to being a hired hand of Midianite shepherds. It was a bizarre turn of fortune indeed, and one that lasted for over forty years. Yet, a remarkable process was also under way during that period. By tending sheep, Moses learned the topography of a region across which he would eventually be called to lead his people. This serendipitous process is a subtle reminder of how mysterious and ingenious are God's ways of taking bad things and turning them to good advantage. In the hands of this alchemist God of Holy Scripture, nothing is ever wasted, and the lead of difficult experiences is often turned into the gold of blessing.

Four slow decades went by and then, one day, Moses encountered something he had never seen before. It was a desert bush aflame. In itself, this was not unusual given the extreme heat of that region. What was remarkable was that the bush continued to burn without being consumed. One of the wonderful things about Moses was that, for all his disappointments, he had not lost his capacity for wonder and curiosity. The Bible says he "turned aside" to examine more closely this unusual phenomenon. When God saw that there was still an openness of spirit in Moses, the Holy One called Moses by name from out of the burning bush and told him to take off his shoes, for the ground on which he stood was holy. God then affirmed that the time had come for Moses to complete what he had tried to do forty years before: "Go down and confront the Pharaoh and demand that he let my people go. I promise to be with you" (Exodus 3:3-12).

It is intriguing to note what had happened to the young idealist in those forty years. Moses had lost most of his brashness and self-confidence, and his first reaction was to recoil and say, "Oh, no, Lord, not me!" I can just envision him adding, "Wait a minute, God, I know this Pharaoh personally. I was in prep school with him. We were even in the same fraternity, and I know how he thinks. He is not about to let this pool of free labor get away for nothing." God's response to Moses might have been something like this: "Look, you wanted to do something for your people. I want to do something for them, too, but I am going to do it with you, not for you. You need to summon all your personal courage to go and confront the Pharaoh. You must do your best to inspire and mobilize the Hebrews, placing all your energies and insights alongside mine in this endeavor. This is going to be a collaborative project involving us all, not my solo performance." As we know from the Bible, the famous Exodus event from Egypt was indeed a joint venture.

This collaborative form of help is the one that God seems to employ most often in becoming "our refuge and our strength, a very present help in time of trouble." Again and again, the Holy One invites us to use our own creativity and resourcefulness in finding solutions to our problems. God honors our maturity by asking us to partner with him in collaboration, rather than allowing us to remain in an infantile stance. Needless to say, this is often a very stretching challenge. I must admit that there is a side of me that prefers the entire struggle to be assumed by someone else. Friends of mine who are counselors tell me that many people come to them and say, in effect, "Fix me without it causing me any pain." They claim that the first therapeutic hurdle that a counselee needs to overcome is acceptance of the counselor's rejection of that invitation. Only then can the counselee commit to real involvement and collaboration as the way to authentic healing.

Robert Farrar Capon illustrates this same point in an amusing story about a sexton in a Jewish synagogue. He came into the rabbi's office one Friday afternoon and he announced, "I am quitting. I am out of here. I resign!" The rabbi said, "How can you do this? You have been one of our most valued employees for thirty years. Why are you acting so impulsively?" The sexton countered, "I will be honest. I do not believe that there is anything to what we are doing here. It is all a sham." The rabbi asked, "How can you say such a thing?" The sexton responded, "I will give you an example. Every Friday afternoon, as the sun is going down and the Sabbath is about to begin, I have gone into our holy space where the ten words of Moses are there on the wall and I have knelt down and prayed, 'Yahweh, Lord of the universe, please help me win the lottery tomorrow night.' I have done this now for thirty years and nothing has ever happened. I have concluded that there is no one on the other end of this praying business." The rabbi said, "I doubt that this is a valid test, but the Sabbath is about to begin. Let me go into the holy space with you and maybe I can discern what the problem is." They went in together and the sexton repeated the request that he had been making for all those years, and from high up in the shadowy eaves of the temple a deep, resonant Voice boomed, "Mosey, Mosey! Give me a break. Buy a ticket!"

This has a touch of slapstick humor in it, but the point is a valid one, for there are many tasks in our world that can be accomplished only through our active participation. Take, for example, the process of learning. My young son used to get frustrated with some of his homework assignments and come to me in tearful distress. What he most wanted was for me to solve the problems and do the homework for him. However, if I had given in to his requests, the whole point of his schooling would have been aborted. There are many experiences in life that come to fulfillment only through collaboration, and this is as true in relation to God as in any other situation. Therefore, in addition to times of miraculous intervention and rescue, it is important to give equal value to the occasions when the Divine One pulls alongside us and inspires us to become active participants in solving our own dilemmas.

God and the Gift of Endurance

The third form of God's "grace to help us in our times of trouble" is the quietest and the most easily overlooked of all. I call it "the gift of endurance." There are times when, for inscrutable reasons, God chooses to solve our problems *for* us. There are other occasions when the Holy One offers to solve our problems *with* us, and then there are those times when God seems to be saying, "There will be no solving of the problem, but I will give you the strength to endure the unchangeable and to experience real growth in the process."

A biblical example of this is Saint Paul's well-known encounter with what he described as his "thorn in the flesh" (2 Corinthians 12:7-10). Some physical malady seemed to cause the great apostle ongoing difficulty. It impeded his work and was a chronic source of irritation. Given the rich vitality of Paul's relationship to God, he did not hesitate to make this problem a repeated object of prayer. Being the practical activist that he was, I am confident that he had also sought the best medical resources to be found in that first-century culture, but to no avail. Finally, it became clear to Paul that God was not going to remove the thorn from him, either by miracle or collaborative measures, but was going to give him the strength to bear it. These were God's words of promise to Paul: "My grace is sufficient for you, for my power is made perfect in weakness" (2 Corinthians 12:9).

In all honesty, this form of "the grace to help us in our times of trouble" is the opposite of what the typical sufferer wants most in a difficult situation. We tend to be very pragmatic when it comes to our hardships; being offered solely the power to endure or merely to "hang in there" is hardly what we have in mind. Nevertheless, I have learned through a very painful period in my own life that the gift of endurance is of immense value.

In July of 1968, I sat in the office of the chief hematologist of Children's Hospital in Louisville, Kentucky, and heard the doctor say words that sent a chill through my whole being. He told me that my eight-and-a-half-year-old daughter was suffering from acute lymphatic leukemia and was critically ill. I was utterly stunned at first. I knew that

Laura Lue had been ill for nearly six weeks, but I had no inkling that the problem was life-threatening. When I recovered from the shock and found my voice, I did what I suppose any concerned parent would have done and asked, "What is her prognosis?" The physician responded in a classical scientific manner. He acknowledged that there was no precise way of anticipating the future, but that the national average for this age child with this particular type of leukemia was eighteen months from diagnosis to death. Needless to say, that was the day the world turned upside down for me. From that moment on, I began to do everything in my power to forestall the ravaging advance of this deadly disease. Literally hundreds of friends began to pray earnestly with me that the One who made this precious child would see fit to mend her little body. I sought the best medical help available in 1968, and I have nothing but boundless gratitude for all that was done for Laura Lue by countless doctors, nurses, and other medical personnel. However, on a snowy Saturday evening in early January of 1970, exactly ten days beyond the eighteen-month projection her doctor had made, the crucial battle was lost, and I stood in wordless agony as the spirit of that little one set out on a journey on which I could not accompany her. It was and remains the single saddest day of my life. I had carried her precious little body back and forth to the bathroom and various hospitals so many times that seeing her move beyond my grasp was overwhelmingly devastating.

In the weeks that followed her death, I went through the dismaying array of emotions that accompany such a great loss. A friend of mine once observed that all grief comes down to this one thing: we run out of time. Something significant ends before we want it to, and that was certainly so in this situation. I was an active pastor while all of this was taking place, and I was so overwhelmed by my grief that I made no effort to resume my duties for weeks. In time, however, as my energies allowed, I slowly resumed some of my pastoral duties. One afternoon, while I was visiting a hospital, I ran into a Jewish rabbi whom I had not seen since Laura Lue's death. He was genuinely empathic as he shared his sorrow with me, but then he startled me by saying, "I want to ask you something, man to man and heart to heart. Did God do anything for you in that stretch of darkness through which you have just come?" In all honesty, I was taken aback by his question. I had not expected that sort of personal and intrusive inquiry at that particular moment. However, as I looked into the burning intensity of his eyes, I realized that here was one of those holy moments when a sincere human being dares to reach out to another and ask, "What was it like in the valley of the shadow of grief? Were there any traces of Divine Presence amid all that pain and anguish? Tell me, please, about the darkness!"

I quickly sensed that this was no occasion for glib shibboleths or a superficial religious exchange. We were suddenly thrust into the realm of life-and-death significance and, because of that, I made no effort to respond immediately. Rather, standing there in the lobby of the hospital, I let my mind wander over the events of the last twenty months. I remembered those times when I thought that I could not bear another instant of the terrible events going on about me. The memory of one morning, in particular, came surging back to me. It was close to the end of Laura Lue's struggles. Most of her veins had collapsed and an intern was trying to begin an intravenous procedure without any success. As he stuck her over and over again, my little daughter pleaded with me to make him stop because it was hurting so much. The tension was so great that I remember thinking, "I simply cannot stand this anymore!" I wanted to run screaming out of that room and never come back. Never before had the pain of my powerlessness been more acute. Yet as the memory of that awful morning came rushing back, I realized something else. From somewhere far beyond me, an Energy not my own had silently enveloped me like a gentle mist and enabled me to resist running away in panic, and to stay connected and be present for my suffering daughter. This was not the only time that I experienced such a gentle sustaining. I finally answered my friend, the rabbi, "Yes, God did do something in the depths of that darkness. God did not do what I most wanted, which, of course, was to heal Laura Lue, nor did God enable the medical establishment to bring about a much desired recovery through their collaboration, but the Holy One was not absent in all that travail. My brave young daughter and I were given the gift of endurance and, along with it, an opportunity to grow spiritually. I cannot begin to describe the incredible maturity and courage that I saw develop in my little one as that disease ravaged her, and yet she never became bitter or lost her love for life. I myself have become a very different person from the one I was before her death. I am not at all proud of this, but for years I took life for granted and assumed that having a healthy family was precisely what I deserved. I see now what an astonishingly good fortune even a single day really is. The realization that life is gift and birth is windfall is more apparent to me than ever before. I sense that I am more humble, grateful, and sensitively attuned to the suffering of others than was the case before this ordeal. As I have said, God did not do what I would have wanted most, but what God did do was a grace of tremendous value, indeed."

It was this terrible stretch of road over thirty years ago that helped me understand this third form of God's "grace to help us in our times of trouble." It also led me to affirm that the secret to a kind of hope that will not disappoint consists in allowing all three of these forms of divine help to constitute one's spectrum of expectations. To repeat a colloquial image, there are many keys on God's keyboard of helpfulness, and accepting the wisdom of the Holy One to use whichever is most appropriate to his purpose is the antidote to disappointment and disillusionment.

As this threefold understanding of God's ways with us began to take shape in my mind, it dawned on me that there was nothing new or original about such a vision.

Many centuries ago, the writer of the book of Isaiah discerned this very pattern in the words that were quoted in the beginning of this chapter: "They who wait upon the LORD shall renew their strength." That is, they will be energized by the action of God in their lives. How will this occur? On occasion, "They shall mount up with wings as eagles." This is the experience of rescue, intervention, and miracle, in which energies from another dimension of reality break in and dramatically alter the shape of our circumstances. At other times, "They shall run and not be weary." We will be accompanied by divine energies and empowered collaboratively to achieve solutions. However, in some situations, what God chooses to do is to give us the grace to "walk and not faint" (Isaiah 40:31). This is the least dramatic of all the Divine's expressions, being given the ability simply to inch along and barely stay on one's feet without collapsing. I once heard an academic critic say that the author of Isaiah seemed to have gotten the sequence wrong because we learn to walk before we can run or even fly. As I listened to him, I thought to myself, "You have obviously never been where I, and millions of other sufferers, have found themselves. I know from experience what it is like to be in a place in which there is no occasion to fly and no room to run and, in such circumstances, the ability to walk and not faint is itself a towering miracle."

One essential component of hope is a belief in the reality of help from beyond oneself. The great good news of Holy Scripture is that the One who made all things genuinely cares about everything that has been created. The heart of the Eternal is wondrously kind and the way to embrace the hope that grows out of such a vision is finally to "let God be God" and allow that One to determine the shape of "the grace to help us in our times of trouble."

CHAPTER FOUR

Hope and Forgiveness

Whenever the word "hope" comes up in conversation, our thoughts instinctively turn toward the future because that is the realm of existence that we commonly associate with this reality. Hope is certainly a stance of positive expectation in relation to the Great Not Yet, a sense that lively and meaningful prospects lie out ahead. For this reason, it may seem puzzling to bring the subject of the past into a discussion of hopefulness, but it is utterly necessary, for we are what has been called "poly-temporal creatures." The way we choose to relate to what has already happened to us exerts a powerful influence on how we handle the not-yet-experienced.

A friend of mine, who is a counselor, often says, "Tell me how you remember, and I will tell you who you are." The old image of "the dead hand of the past" is an erroneous one. There is nothing "dead" about our memories. The contemporary psychologist Lewis Smedes turns an old adage about memory on its head. Instead of the familiar "Forgive and forget," Smedes says that we need to learn to forgive and be forgiven because we cannot forget. He refers to that mysterious capacity of recall over which we do not exercise complete control. Think of the times, in the middle of the night or at some unguarded moment, when scenes from the past come flooding into our consciousness unbidden. These memories are an important component of our everyday experiences, and the role we allow them to play in shaping our expectations has a powerful impact on whether we view the future as a beckoning friend or a menacing foe.

When we are talking about the past, a profound awareness of God's everlasting mercy is utterly essential to the kind of hope that will not disappoint. In one of the most beloved prayers in the Anglican Book of Common Prayer, often referred to as the Prayer of Humble Access, God is described as One "whose property is always to have mercy"

(BCP, 337). This particular quality is crucial, given the sordid performance of our species throughout the history of this planet. There are few things about us humans that can be described as truly universal, but one constant is that none of us has done life perfectly! Saint Paul was right in saying that "all have sinned and fall short of the glory of God" (Romans 3:23). It is too late for any of us to worry about innocence. We all have skeletons in our closets, memories of things we have done that we wish we had not done, and just as many things we did not do that we wish we had. There is enough in all of our backgrounds to make us blush deeply with regret.

Nevertheless, a great spiritual danger lies in allowing memories of our failures to cause us to slip into despair. I know of nothing more potent to counter such a threat than the vision of the endless patience and radical mercy of the Holy One. Madeleine L'Engle, in her wonderful novel *A Live Coal in the Sea*, echoes the same vision in the beautiful words of an ancient mystic who wrote, "All the evil that human beings have ever conceived or done is no more to the mercy of God than a live coal to the sea." Here are the true proportions of God's mercy and human sinfulness set in vivid contrast.

One of the most powerful descriptions of the effects of such a vision is found in an experience that the late Arthur Gordon recounted in his moving book *A Touch of Wonder*.[1] Gordon was born and raised in Savannah, Georgia, and he went on to become an honor graduate of Yale University and a Rhodes scholar. He settled into a literary career in New York City following World War II, but he hit a stretch of personal setbacks in the late 1940s that thrust him into a state of deep depression. He had a close friend who was an eminent psychiatrist and, one wintry afternoon, young Gordon made an appointment to meet with him. When the counselor inquired as to what was troubling Gordon, he described in detail his many regrets—all the mistakes he had made, his moments of bad judgment and missed opportunities. After several minutes of nothing but agonizing laments, the psychiatrist said, "I want you to listen to something. I want to get your reactions." With that, he took a tape out of a box and put it into a machine. He explained, "These are three short recordings made by people who came to me for help. I have their permission to use this material. I want you to listen and see if you can pick out the two-word phrase that is the common denominator in all three cases."

As Gordon listened, the one thing the three seemed to have in common was their profound unhappiness. The first man who spoke had obviously suffered some sort of business failure and was berating himself for not working harder or more wisely. The second was a woman who had never married because of pressures from her family, and she was thoroughly embittered over all the marital opportunities she had let slip by. The third voice belonged to a mother whose teenage child was in trouble with the police and she blamed herself. When the psychiatrist turned off the machine, he said, "Six times in these recordings a phrase was used that is full of subtle poison. Did you spot it? Probably not, because you used it three times yourself a few minutes ago." With that, the psychiatrist picked up the box that held the tape and said, "The poisonous words are right there on the label, the two saddest words in any language." Gordon looked down and printed neatly in red ink were the two words, "If only. . . ." The counselor then continued, "You would be surprised by how many thousands of times I have sat in this chair and listened to woeful sentences that began with those two words. The problem is that these words do not change anything. They keep a person facing the wrong way—backwards instead of forward.

They are a waste of time. In the end, if you let this image grow into a habit, it becomes a real roadblock, for it provides one with an excuse for not trying anymore. Now take your own case: Your plans did not work out. Why? Because you made certain mistakes. Well, that's all right: Everyone makes mistakes. Mistakes are what we learn from. But when you were telling me about them, lamenting this, regretting that, you weren't really learning from them . . . because you never got out of the past tense. Not once did you mention the future. And in a way. . . you were enjoying it. There's a perverse streak in all of us that makes us like to hash over old mistakes. After all, when you relate the story of some disaster or disappointment . . . you're still the chief character, still in the center of the stage."

When Gordon asked for a remedy, the counselor told him he needed to shift his focus by changing the keywords he was using. He suggested replacing the words "If only" with the phrase "Next time." He told Gordon of seeing minor miracles occur right there in his office when people start assuming this stance in relation to their bad memories. While we cannot go back and undo it or relive the past, we can resolve not to let the wisdom it can provide from being wasted on us. Focusing on what to do next time is deciding to act differently in the future in light of what one has learned from the past. It is turning a roadblock into a stepping-stone. As young Gordon pondered what his friend told him, he said it was as if something very basic clicked in his mind and he felt himself undergoing a genuine shift of perspective that lasted for the rest of his life. While no specific theological images were used in describing this profound change of viewpoint, such an event is wholly consistent with the image of God that emerges from the pages of Holy Scripture. Qualities such as unconditional love, everlasting mercy, and unlimited patience are repeatedly attributed to the Holy One, and facilitating a new way of letting the past interact with the future is exactly what you would expect from this kind of Being.

Jesus embodied these attributes and this way of looking to the future. While teaching in front of the Temple in Jerusalem one day, he was interrupted by an excited group of men with a disheveled-looking woman in their midst. They explained that they had just caught her in the act of adultery and they wanted to know what Jesus thought should be done to her. It was an awkward and provocative moment. Jesus realized they were trying to put him—and the woman—on the spot. He deftly redirected them by saying, "He who is without sin, let him be the first to cast a stone of judgment." It was a reminder that no finite human being has either the knowledge or the virtue to occupy the "judgment seat." Only God is capable of such an action. It is to their credit that, when the issue was framed this way, the accusers recognized that they were not "without sin" and quietly stole away.

Then Jesus faced the frightened woman and asked tenderly, "Is there no one to accuse you?" She replied, "No one, Sir." Jesus uttered what must have been blessed music to her ears when he said, "Neither do I condemn you. Go and sin no more" (John 8:2-11). What is this but another example of shifting the focus from an "if only" kind of lamenting to a "next time" form of hopefulness? The image of the Holy One found in this event is rich and potent indeed. I have a clear sense that God is more interested in a person's future than in his or her past, and has more concern for what a person can yet become than what he or she used to be. The phrase "Neither do I condemn you" meant that Jesus refused to imprison the woman in her past, that part of existence that cannot be altered.

I think that many of our difficulties could be resolved by embracing a single truth: The present is not the past! This is exactly what Jesus was saying to the woman, and the same is true for us. The One who knows everything that we have ever done has not given up on us, and the future offers fresh opportunities. Jesus' words, "Go and sin no more," are certainly not those of a perfectionist who promotes the belief that one strike means you're out. Jesus seems to be saying that the pain caused by misusing one's energies needs to be taken seriously, and we should learn what the past has to teach us rather than letting it be wasted on us. I believe it is safe to say that the God of Holy Scripture is more interested in what we have learned from our mistakes than the fact that we have made them.

There is no finer reflection of God's essence than what the prophet Jeremiah saw when he was inspired to go to the shop of a potter one day. As he observed the work of this artist, Jeremiah was moved by the exquisite patience and wisdom in the potter's unhurriedly working and reworking of the lump of clay until it was finally fashioned into a lovely vase. Then the prophet heard God say, "Can I not do with you, O house of Israel, as this potter has done? Just like the clay is in the potter's hand, so are you in my hand, O house of Israel" (Jeremiah 18:5-6). This understanding of how the Merciful One has chosen to deal with human imperfection is a crucial element of a hopeful perspective.

The God of the Bible is clearly not a demanding perfectionist who will tolerate only the blameless and the spotless. However, one passage of Scripture seems to contradict this and that is the text that is usually translated, "Be ye therefore perfect, as your Father in heaven is perfect" (Matthew 5:48). When I learned that in Greek the future and the imperative tenses are spelled exactly alike, I realized that this verse is a promise, not a commandment, and it should be rendered, "You *shall* be perfect, even as your Father in heaven is perfect." This means that God always seeks to move us toward completeness and wholeness. If perfection were viewed as a prerequisite before God will have anything to do with us, there would be no hope for us. However, if this is a goal toward which all of God's merciful energies are directed, genuine hope becomes not only a possibility, but also a process in which we can confidently participate.

Why, then, in light of such a grace, do so many people choose to live outside this circle of hopefulness? I have been puzzled for a long time about this question and I can only conclude that the problem has to do with the issue of

egocentricity. When we experience an event of genuine forgiveness, there is everything for which to be grateful but
nothing of which to be proud. The gift of God's mercy cuts
squarely across the arrogance of our egos. What we have to
acknowledge is that all of life is ultimately a gift, which
means that gratitude, trust, and humility are the appropriate responses, rather than pride or self-sufficiency. It is very
threatening to have to admit that, spiritually speaking, we
are all "on welfare," but this is the deepest truth. What John
the Baptist said after encountering Jesus of Nazareth is
what all of us are called on to say to the mercy of God: "He
must increase, but I must decrease" (John 3:30). The grace
of God must become the source of our final hope, rather
than the things we have done or failed to do.

I have come to the conclusion that an experience of
God's forgiveness is more akin to birth than anything else.
It comes out of God's willingness to give us second chances
at life, on the same terms that we were given our first
chance at birth. None of us did anything to earn our way
into this wonder of aliveness. Our entrance into history was
sheer windfall, and the same is true of an experience of
God's mercy. It is rooted finally in what God is, rather than
in what we do. Trusting in that particular understanding of

the nature of God is what enables us to turn from a preoccupation with what might have been "if only" something had been different, to a grateful and confident hopefulness about "next time."

The writer Frederick Buechner was well into his twenties before this vision of the Holy One became a living event for him. He was reared in a family that did not go to church, and was educated at the Lawrenceville School and Princeton University without any significant spiritual encounters during that time. He experienced great success when he published his first novel. However, in the late 1950s his fortunes turned and he found himself floundering, both personally and professionally. A friend invited him to start attending a church on Madison Avenue where a pulpit giant named George Buttrick was the senior minister. Through this man's preaching, young Buechner experienced an authentic religious epiphany one Sunday. To use a vernacular expression, "God happened to him" in a vibrant, existential way. As a result, Buechner decided to explore more deeply the sources from which Buttrick's vision emerged, and he began to study at Union Theological Seminary in Manhattan. It was there that this gifted young writer first encountered the documents of Holy Scripture.

Buechner reported being astonished by the earthy realism and honesty of the Bible. It was by no means a kind of *Barlett's Collection of Familiar Quotations,* as he had supposed. Even more surprising to Buechner was a motif that he found again and again in the Great Story: the seemingly worst things are never the last things in the hands of God's ingenious mercy. The Holy One always seemed to have something surprising "up his sleeve," like master chess players who are never outflanked by an opponent because they always counter with a strategy to advance their advantage. Buechner discovered this pattern throughout the Old Testament, and sensed it coming to its climax in the Easter event on the heels of Good Friday. This realization, that the worst things are never the last things with this alchemist God, forms the basic foundation for an outlook of hopefulness. It offers the most potent resource I know to break the deadly spell of pessimism and despair. Given what we know from the revelation of Holy Scripture, God is the ultimate source of hope. In his gracious hands, it can be said that God's goodness is bigger than all human badness, and

God's power to redeem is finally greater than evil's power to corrupt.

NOTE

1. Arthur Gordon, *A Touch of Wonder* (Old Tappen, N. J.: Fleming H. Revell Company, 1974), 68–72.

CHAPTER FIVE

Hope and the Life to Come

That legendary Old Testament sufferer named Job put into words many centuries ago a question that probably has crossed the minds of most people at one time or another. Job's question, "If a man dies, will he live again? (Job 14:14), echoes ours. Most of us cannot help but wonder what lies beyond the event of our last breath, but we have no actual experience from which to draw an answer. Though some have told of what are called "near-death experiences," none of us has traversed that very last boundary and come back to share a witness. Death remains a paradoxical "certain uncertainty": We know it is going to happen eventually to us all, yet we do not know exactly what it is going to be like.

This lack of evidence has led many to a position of agnosticism about the whole subject. The writer Philip Simmons, who is himself dying slowly of Lou Gehrig's disease, admits very honestly, "I do not know what, if anything, follows this life. Certain scenarios are appealing to me: reunion with my childhood pets, all-night jam sessions with Jerry Garcia, reincarnation as a basset hound. But none of that may come to pass. I do not mean to discount belief in an afterlife or in reincarnation, or the comfort and moral discipline such beliefs can provide. But these are matters of faith, not knowledge in the scientific or rational sense and, as such, are better left to the individual conscience."[1]

Simmons's position is a very honest and cautious one to take, but it falls sadly short of that hope for which our hearts hunger. Saint Paul observed long ago, "If, in this life only, we have hope in Christ, then we of all humans are most to be pitied" (1 Corinthians 15:19). I find myself agreeing with his sentiments, for any authentic discussion of "a hope that will not disappoint" must include some reflection on that mysterious realm of existence that lies beyond the grave. Simmons is quite right in saying that knowledge of this sort is neither scientific nor rational, but there is another resource that affords us profound insight, namely, what we have come to know from allowing Holy Scripture to illumine our minds and hearts. It is to that sacred source that we must turn for this form of hopefulness, and it can make a vast difference on our basic outlook when we do so.

Many people consider the late Eugene O'Neill the finest American playwright of the twentieth century. By no means was his personal life an easy one—a fact reflected in the title of his autobiographical masterpiece, *A Long Day's Journey Into Night*. It was his honest conclusion that the final shape of the human saga is a decline into nothingness. Another gifted interpreter, whose life experiences were also tumultuous, came to the opposite conclusion in a much earlier time. Saint Paul believed that life is finally more like a long night's journey into day. He says as much in 1 Corinthians 13: "For our knowledge is imperfect and our prophecy is imperfect; but when the perfect comes, the imperfect will pass away. . . . Now we see through a glass darkly, but then face to face. Now I know in part; then I shall understand fully, even as I have been fully understood" (1 Corinthians 13:9, 12). The contrast between these two visions is striking, and what accounts for the difference between them is the impact of the Great Story of Holy Scripture.

What is the essence of this revelation? It can be stated quite simply: God is love, only love, and nothing but love; and one of the primal characteristics of this love is the fact that it is eternal. We have already spoken of the generosity that was at work in the initial act of creation, and was by no means a thoughtless or irresponsible act on the part of the Holy One. What God chose to create, God also loved intensely. Does not Genesis depict God as exuding delight again and again as he viewed the works of his own hands? "It is good! It is good! It is very, very good!" are the words that echo throughout the whole first chapter of that book. It follows that the Creator continued to take seriously what had been called into being through God's own intentionality.

There was nothing temporary or frivolous about the affection of the Holy One. God did not relate to creation in the manner of a child, who might make toy soldiers, wind them up, play with them for a while, and then lose interest in them. I remember certain Christmas mornings, when my two children were very young. It was nearly impossible to get them to sleep on Christmas Eve but, long before the sun came up, they were excitedly opening all of their packages under the Christmas tree. Yet, amazingly, before the sun went down on that same day, I can recall their saying petulantly, "What can we play with? There's nothing interesting to do. We're bored!" God's love is not like the short-spanned affection of little children. What God creates, God loves and what God loves, God loves everlastingly. In the same famous passage from which I just quoted, Saint Paul makes this point vividly by affirming that "Love bears all things, believes all things, hopes all things, endures all things. Love never ends" (1 Corinthians 13:7-8). This quality of God's eternal love is the foundation of the hope that our life with the Holy One will not end when the physical phase of our lives is over.

People often ask me, "What is it like to die?" I have to be honest and say, "I have not yet had that experience, so I cannot give you a firsthand description, but I can share what I have gleaned from my own life and from the pages of Holy Scripture." I believe that what happens to us at the end of our lives on earth is very much like what happens at the beginning. We all start out as two tiny cells in our mothers' bodies. Consider how extraordinary it is that a particular sperm would interact with a particular egg at just the fortuitous moment when a new organism could be formed, and this is precisely what happens at conception. From that infinitesimally small beginning, a fetus grows and develops in marvelous ways. The womb is a wonderfully appropriate place for this sort of process, complete with round-the-clock room service and a desirable temperature. Yet, a trauma of separation occurs after about thirty-eight weeks that, from the vantage point of the womb, is a kind of death. The fetus leaves the protective and nurturing context that has made its development possible and is suddenly thrust into a radically different environment. From the vantage point of time and space, however, that same event is described as birth.

Thus, death and birth are really two sides of the same coin. Dying to one thing that we might be born to another seems to be the way that God gives us access to his kind of joy. Life comes to us in increments, and the process of letting go of what has served its purpose opens the way for us to enter into a realm of even grander promise. Think of the many ways that we can develop that would have been impossible had we stayed embedded in our mother's womb. We experience this pattern—this death and birth—again and again in the saga of a normal human life. Just as we "die" to the womb in order to be "born" into this world, we subsequently "die" to the swings and sand pile of the backyard in order to be "born" to the world of school. We "die" to elementary school that we may be "born" to junior high school, and so the pattern continues. A friend of mine once put it this way: "Every exit is also an entrance. We never walk out of one thing into complete nothingness. There is always an arena of greater possibilities out ahead of us." This understanding of the way the Holy One has chosen to fulfill his purpose is the basis for believing that new levels of existence await us when "the dark at the end of the tunnel" opens into ever grander light.

The passage of Scripture used most frequently in Christian funerals affirms this basic hope. In the beginning of John 14, Jesus says, "Let not your hearts be troubled; believe in God, believe also in me. In my Father's house are many dwelling places; if it were not so, would I have told you that I go to prepare a place for you? When I go and prepare a place for you, I will come again and will take you to myself, that where I am, there you may be also" (John 14:1-3). Here is the clear declaration that there are worlds beyond this world of time and space, other schoolrooms, if you please, where the task of learning to love God, our neighbors, and ourselves can take place more fully. Added to this vision is the blessed promise that, contrary to that sad old spiritual, we will *not* have to "walk that lonesome valley" by ourselves. The One who "for us and our salvation came down from heaven" has said, in effect, "I will not forget you or abandon you. When you breathe your last breath, I promise to meet you and accompany you to the next realm. Did not I give you my word long ago, 'Lo, I will be with you always, even to the end of the world' (Matthew 28:20)? Trust that above all else."

I once heard a touching story that makes this point in a lovely way. A little boy was dying slowly of cancer. As a way of diverting his attention from his pain, his mother spent long hours reading to him. One afternoon, as they shared a story about King Arthur and his knights, the lad startled his mother with the question, "What is it like to die, Mama? Does it hurt?" These words caught his mother off guard, but as she looked into his eyes, she realized that his was not an expression of idle curiosity. More often than not, the dying sense that they are dying, and all the accounts in the book about knights fighting and dying had brought that dark possibility to the surface of the child's consciousness. Tears welled in the mother's eyes, and she excused herself on the pretext of having to check on something in the kitchen. However, the space there between the refrigerator and the sink quickly became a temple of sorts. She looked toward heaven and said, "Please, God, please give me a way to answer my child's question and lessen the terror I see in his face." In that moment, the kitchen became a holy space, and an answer was supplied. She dried her tears and went back in and said, "You asked me a minute ago what it is like to die. Well, do you remember, before you were sick, how you used to play outdoors all day? You would come in, eat supper, and then sit down on the couch in the den to watch television and fall fast asleep. The next morning you would be surprised to wake up in your bed with your pajamas on. What you did not know was that your big brother, who loves you very much, had gently picked you up and taken you upstairs, put your night-clothes on you and tucked you in. That is what it is like to die. You go to sleep in one room of God's house and you wake up in another; and the way that you get from one place to the other is in the strong arms of our loving Brother, Jesus Himself." This image settled deeply into the lad's understanding and, a few weeks later, when it came time for him to make the Great Transition, he did so without fear.

Nothing could express the heart of the Christian hope for the life to come more simply or beautifully than this little story. A wise mentor of mine once said, "When I die, I will get to the place that I will have to say, 'If there is anything else, it is up to God.' I will be a spent arrow, a being with no force or potency left whatsoever. I believe we were put here in this schoolroom of time and space to have enough experiences of God's love and mercy so that, when we have to lie down in total helplessness, we will not lie down in fearfulness but in hope and trust."

What I have been saying in this volume was lived out graphically when one of the great souls of the twentieth century came to the end of his earthly journey. I referred before to Clarence Jordan, who single-handedly founded a unique Christian community in rural Georgia called Koinonia Farms in the 1940s. This is the entity out of which has grown the worldwide enterprise now known as Habitat for Humanity. Jordan was the recognized spiritual leader of that community for many decades. Like the little boy with cancer, the time came when he realized that he was dying, and he proceeded to leave detailed instructions for how his funeral service was to be conducted. His final request was to be buried simply in a pine coffin at a particular spot on the farm he had come to love so dearly. The one issue he had not addressed was what should be said at the gravesite. The burial service unfolded just as he had planned, but when the community gathered around the designated grave, an awkward silence settled over the group. Jordan had always been the one to offer leadership in such a situation and now he was gone. A three-year-old girl, who had loved Jordan very much, must have recognized the awkwardness of that poignant moment and, quite spontaneously, she stepped up to the casket and began to sing her favorite song. "Happy Birthday to you! Happy Birthday to you! Happy Birthday, dear Clarence, Happy Birthday to you!" Jordan's biographer observed that there could not have been a more appropriate ending to a remarkable Christian life. That story also embodies the essence of a hope that will not disappoint. Our death day will also be our birthday into eternal life, as many of us affirm every Sunday in the magnificent words of the Nicene Creed, "We look for the resurrection of the dead, and the life of the world to come." I end these reflections with the prayer that your journey into all that lies ahead will not be one of fear, but one of great joy and abundant hope. Let it be, dear God, let it be!

NOTE

1. Philip Simmons, *Learning to Fall: The Blessing of Our Imperfect Life* (New York: Bantam Books, 2002), 146.

About the Author

John R. Claypool was born in Franklin, Kentucky, and was reared in Nashville, Tennessee. He received his undergraduate degree in philosophy from Baylor University in Waco, Texas, and his theological training at Southern Baptist Seminary in Louisville, Kentucky, and the Episcopal Theological Seminary of the Southwest in Austin, Texas. Dr. Claypool earned a doctorate in theology and has received four honorary doctor's degrees. He was ordained to ministry in 1953 and served as pastor of five Baptist churches in Kentucky, Tennessee, Texas, and Mississippi. He was ordained an Episcopal priest in 1986 and served as rector of Saint Luke's Episcopal Church in

Birmingham, Alabama, for nearly fourteen years. Since 2001 he has served as theologian-in-residence at Trinity Episcopal Church in New Orleans, Louisiana, and as Visiting Professor of Homiletics at Mercer University's McAfee School of Theology in Atlanta, Georgia. Dr. Claypool and his wife, Ann, have three children and two grandchildren.